Lukas Fiedler

The Transformation of Industrial Sites to Recreational Areas - in Duisburg

Examples: RheinPark and Heinrich-Hildebrand-Höhe

GRIN Verlag

Bibliografische Information der Deutschen Nationalbibliothek:

Die Deutsche Bibliothek verzeichnet diese Publikation in der Deutschen National-
bibliografie; detaillierte bibliografische Daten sind im Internet über http://dnb.d-
nb.de/ abrufbar.

Imprint:

Copyright © 2009 GRIN Verlag GmbH
Druck und Bindung: Books on Demand GmbH, Norderstedt Germany
ISBN: 978-3-640-75946-0

This book at GRIN:

http://www.grin.com/en/e-book/161015/the-transformation-of-industrial-sites-to-
recreational-areas-in-duisburg

GRIN - Your knowledge has value

Der GRIN Verlag publiziert seit 1998 wissenschaftliche Arbeiten von Studenten, Hochschullehrern und anderen Akademikern als eBook und gedrucktes Buch. Die Verlagswebsite www.grin.com ist die ideale Plattform zur Veröffentlichung von Hausarbeiten, Abschlussarbeiten, wissenschaftlichen Aufsätzen, Dissertationen und Fachbüchern.

Visit us on the internet:

http://www.grin.com/

http://www.facebook.com/grincom

http://www.twitter.com/grin_com

Reinhard und Max Mannesmann Gymnasium Duisburg

FACHARBEIT
im Grundkurs Geographie Bilingual

The Transformation of Industrial Sites to Recreational Areas - in Duisburg. Examples: RheinPark and Heinrich-Hildebrand-Höhe

Verfasser: Lukas Fiedler

Jahrgangstufe: 12

Bearbeitungszeit: 5 Wochen

Abgabetermin: 14.12.2009

Table of Contents

1. Introduction

This essay will be about the transformation of industrial sites to recreational areas in Duisburg. This will be done by taking a closer look on the projects "Heinrich Hildebrand-Höhe" and "RheinPark". These two projects were chosen because they are relatively young projects and are located in the author's hometown.

For the given information concerning the two projects I mainly took into consideration current sources like newspaper articles, brochures by the city of Duisburg and articles from the Internet, mainly from news pages. Regarding Duisburg's industrial history I concentrated on books that could easily be found in the municipal library of Duisburg.

The topic was chosen due to the fact that I noticed more and more recreational areas emerging on former industrial ground in my immediate surroundings. This is the reason why I got interested in these projects. I wanted to know why and how they were built in a more detailed way than I already knew from newspapers and other media.

The essay is basically divided into three parts. First there is this introduction to introduce in my ways of working on the topic. In the second part there will be an overview on the industrial development in Duisburg to make the need of transforming industrial areas better understandable. After that the aims and ways of the transformation from industry to recreation will be presented using the examples of the future designing program "IBA Emscher Park". Thereafter, in the third part, information on the two projects from this essay's title in Duisburg will be given in a more detailed way.

In the case of Heinrich-Hildebrand-Höhe I also put the emphasis on the history of the area and ground due to the importance concerning the contemporary use. Regarding RheinPark I did not concentrate on that aspect because it does not affect today's use in a considerable way.

Finally there will be a conclusion on the topic highlighting advantages and disadvantages for the place of location Duisburg and for Duisburg's inhabitants.

2. The industrial Development of Duisburg

Duisburg's latest History is strongly connected to the changes in the Industry. It rose beginning in the mid 19th century due to the industrial revolution, had its most flourishing years in the 1950s and 1960s and began to shrink beginning in the 1970s until today.

2.1 Rise of Industry in Duisburg

Duisburg's steel industry began to rise in the mid 19th century when more and more railways were built. These railways were the basis of Duisburg's success in steel production. The good connections to the rivers Rhine and Ruhr were also an argument to set up the industrial facilities in Duisburg[1]. Also the considerable coal and iron ore resources were a clear advantage of Duisburg[1].All these locational factors made big steel companies like Krupp and Thyssen settle down in Duisburg.

In opposite to other cities of the Ruhr Area the industrial rise was not mainly triggered by mining but also by the chemical industry. Already in 1824 the first German sulfuric acid factory was set up in Duisburg-Kasslerfeld which constituted the rise of the chemical large scale industry[2].

To satisfy the need of coal for the steel production mining companies evolved beginning in 1850. In 1866, 490 miners in one mine extracted 800t stone coal a day[3].

Indeed chemical production took place in the industrializing Duisburg, however the steel and mining industries were dominating[3].

2.2 Structural Change concerning Industry

After the industrial facilities had been rebuilt successfully very rapidly after World War II, Duisburg's economy was in a really good condition. Due to the "Wirtschaftswunder"-years (the 1950s) the production and employment increased significantly. From 1950 to 1958 35.000 new jobs were created in industrial companies. The total

---

1   Müller 2000
2   Roden 1975, S. 187f

number was 105.000 employees in 1958[3]. Duisburg was economically very strong at that time. The GDP in 1957 was 48% higher than in the whole of Germany.

Beginning in 1957 the situation began to change, initiated by the coal crisis. Because of an increasing importance of oil and gas coal began to lose its importance. This fact led to the closing of multiple mines.

The high steel demand compensated that development. There were still enough jobs in the steel production branch.

Beginning in the 1970s until today a huge steel crisis took place. Due to the fact that the German government prohibited the import of foreign coal whereas German coal was too expensive to be used for profitable steel production, Duisburg's steel output declined.

In other European countries high subsidies were given for non profitable steel production facilities whereas German steel companies received only a very small amount of money by the state. In 1980 steel companies in other European countries, like France, Italy and Belgium, received 206 to 235 Deutsche Mark per ton rolled steel. German rolled steel was only subsidized with 17 DM per ton.[4]

Duisburg as well suffered from the worldwide decreasing demand for steel and the worldwide decreasing transport costs and as a consequence of that more companies ordering coal from elsewhere. Also the increasing costs for environmental issues and wages, made it hard for Duisburg to compete[4].

The aim of rise in productivity and the improvement of competitiveness made many high ovens close. In 1986, there were only 42.000 people still working in the steel sector. This number decreased significantly until today. At the present point of time only 20.000 people work in the steel branch[5].

The negative development in the steel industry also caused the loss of jobs and insolvencies in supplier companies. This situation caused a high unemployment rate and a high number of vacant industrial facilities in Duisburg.

---

3   Heid, Kraume, Lerch, Milz, Pietsch, Tromnau, Vinschen 1996, S.372f
4   Ausschuss für Öffentlichkeitsarbeit der Niederrheinischen Industrie und Handelskammer Duisburg 1987, S.57f
5   Hofritz 2004

2.3 The Transformation of industrial Facilities to recreational Areas

Due to the fact that more and more vacant industrial facilities came to existence, the question how to cope with these unused areas arose. An important establishment with the aim to transform vacant industrial areas was the future designing program "IBA Emscher Park" (International building exposition/ Internationale Bauausstellung) that took place in the Ruhr Area from 1989 to 1999[6]. Its main aim was to improve the living standard and residence conditions and resulting from that the image of the region and the 17 affected cities located along the Ruhr. Two of the seven more particular goals were the preservation of industrial sites and the creation of new forms of living.

In the context of the "IBA Emscher Park" 120 projects took place concerning social, cultural, commercial, urbanistic and landscaping topics. These projects were seen as a model for later use also in other regions.[7]

To form an attraction for tourists and inhabitants of the Ruhr Area the "Route der Industriekultur" (route of industrial culture) was established. This itinerary connected important projects of the IBA.

One of these important projects was for example "Landschaftspark Duisburg-Nord". It consists of 200ha areal of industrial facilities like high ovens, that was transformed into an industrial museum and a place for different leisure amenities and sports. Visitors can frequent the original places where in former times employees worked and get an impression how this was like. They also can dive in an old gas container that is now filled up with water or climb on parts of the old facilities. In the summer there is even an open air cinema in the Landschaftspark Nord. To increase the attractiveness the high ovens are illuminated at night[12].

Landschaftspark Duisburg-Nord also was responsible for the creation of many new jobs like gardeners and guides.

Another IBA project located in Duisburg is "Innenhafen Duisburg" (inland harbor Duisburg). An area characterized by vacant grain reservoirs was transformed into a

---

6   Ministerium für Städtebau und Wohnen, Kultur und Sport des Landes Nordrhein-Westfalen
7   Fuchs 1999, S. 46

multi functional place with service, business, residential and leisure function. Discos, restaurants, offices and residential areas located around the water are typical for this project.[8]

These projects are only two examples of multiple projects where old industrial facilities were reconstructed pursuing the goal to create an innovative ambiance with profit for the people and without giving away the facility's old identity.

---

8   Gatermann

3 RheinPark and Heinrich-Hildebrand-Höhe

RheinPark and Heinrich-Hildebrand-Höhe are two non IBA projects. However there are some similarities concerning illumination, leisure amenities and sports possibilities. Both projects are located in the city of Duisburg and on former industrial ground.

3.1 Information concerning RheinPark

RheinPark is a project that was realized from 2006 to 2009 in Duisburg Hochfeld. It consists of an area of 60 hectares of size and of 1,4km of the eastern waterside of the river Rhine. Its main aim is to grant access to the Rhine both to people living in Hochfeld and in the whole of Duisburg and providing a high recreational value. The area had been used for industrial purposes for 150 years before.

Hochfeld has always been located near the Rhine but the population never had had the possibility to enjoy the recreational effect of the river due to the industry at the waterside. The city planers wanted to change that[10]. RheinPark is one of the projects of the "www.duisburg" ("wirtschaft-wohnen-wasser"/economy-living-water) initiative. The initiative's goal is the improvement of economic conditions and the attractiveness of the city of Duisburg.[9]

Today the RheinPark offers multiple leisure amenities e.g. benches, a skate park (see Fig. 1), a climbing wall (see Fig. 2), a streetball court, beach volleyball courts, breakdance stages, playgrounds (see Fig. 3) etc.[10]

3.1.1 Ways of forming the RheinPark

The plans for structuring the Project were excogitated by the "Atelier Loidl und TOPOS" from Berlin. The institution had won an architecture competition that had taken place throughout Europe[10].

In December 2006 workers began tearing down the old industrial facilities of the area aside from the factory premises of ArcelorMittal Hochfeld GmbH (see Fig. 4). The company plans moving to Duisburg-Ruhrort in the future. As this is done, the 18ha

---

9   Stadt Duisburg 2005
10   Duisburg.de A 2008

area will also be torn down and restructured.

However not all parts of the industrial facilities were removed. Some parts were left in order to be a reminder of the industrial past of the area (see Fig. 2). One noticeable element of these remaining, is the old water tower (see Fig. 5). It will be used as a restaurant and as a look-out for people interested in the Rhine and the floodplains on the western side of the Rhine[11].

When the area was cleared in May 2007 workers began to pile up 280.000t of soil to small, flat dumps, so called meadow plateaus ("Wiesenschollen") (see Fig. 6) that had a height up to 6m. These plateaus were built in order to give the park a more structured and attractive look and to give visitors the ability to see the Rhine from many places in the park. 200.000t of the used soil came from the RheinPark and were just rearranged whereas 80.000t were brought from the "Parallelkanal-Project" in Duisburg-Wedau.

After finishing the piling up process the plateaus were grassed and 2.862 trees (Fig. 7) were planted in the whole plot. Between the plateaus a road system was built in deeply engraved channels.

Due to the fact that there is a railway running through the park that is still used, two pedestrian bridges (see Fig. 8) were built over it to increase the accessibility of the park and of the waterside for visitors coming from Duisburg-Hochfeld. Visitors are also able to use the preserved undercrossings (see Fig. 9) to pass under the railway.

For recreation reasons a beach of 300m length was established (see Fig. 10). It consists of a former loading ramp that was filled up with sand. On the beach wooden plateaus, chairs and benches were placed.

To protect visitors from the danger of falling into the Rhine a railing was installed along the waterside.

As an attraction mainly for the younger visitors multiple leisure amenities like skate parks and playgrounds were formed. In the meantime the skate park is very well known, also in outlying regions, and frequently used.

In order to improve the outer appearance of the wall dividing RheinPark and the

---

11   Duisburg.de B

business area of ArcelorMittal and leading the provisional path from Hochfeld to the park, 1400 portraits of citizens of Duisburg were hung up forming the lettering "Duisburg am Rhein"[9] (See Fig. 11).

The first part of RheinPark was opened in September 2008 and costed 37 Mio. Euro. It was financed by the European Union, the department for environment, agriculture and consumer protection of NRW (Ministerium für Umwelt und Naturschutz, Landwirtschaft und Verbraucherschutz) and the NRW department for traffic and manufacturing (Ministerium für Bauen und Verkehr)[9].

3.1.2 Future Plans for RheinPark

The project RheinPark is not finished yet. Some extensions are planned.

A pier is planned to allow the access to the park from the Rhine. This would improve the accessibility of the park and defang the bad parking lot situation[9].

When the ArcelorMittal company has moved away, a situation that will occur later as it was plannned due to the current economic crisis, another 18ha of industrial area will be restructured and transformed to a part of RheinPark. On this part and also on other parts the designers plan to build up different kinds of residential areas and high quality services[9].

For designing these different functional areas the park was divided in three zones (see Fig. 13).

When the project Rhine park is be finished (the date is unknown due to the problems with ArcelorMittal that will move away later as it was planned) the park will be a place for living, trading, recreation, culture, sports, calling on services and of prestige for the city of Duisburg. It is one of the most eminent projects of the upcoming period of time for Duisburg and the region around[10].

3.2. Information concerning Heinrich-Hildebrand-Höhe

Heinrich-Hildebrand-Höhe is a project that was realized from September 2006 to November 2008. It is located in Duisburg-Wanheim-Angerhausen in an area today called "Angerpark". In former times the areal belonged to the copper-producing company "Berzelius Metallhütten AG "

It basically consists of a 67m high dump of 450.000t soil. The material is partly excavation from a regatta course expansion project called "Parallelkanal" that took place in Duisburg-Wedau.

The reason for building this edifice was to not primary to create a recreational area but to keep away dangerous brownfields, that are located in the upper ground, from the groundwater[12].

3.2.1 History of the Berzelius Areal

The smeltery in Wanheim-Angerhausen was founded in 1905. It produced sulfuric acid and copper. In 1906 a zinc production facility was added. In 1926 the Berzelius Smeltery company took over the complex before it was overtaken by the Swiss Sudamin Group in 2002. Under the leadership of the Sudamin Group the complex went bankrupt in 2005, 100 years after foundation.

From 1906 to 2005 the facility produced zinc, copper, lead, tin and other materials. Except for the last few years, before Sudamin Group overtook the facility, the smeltery never worked efficiently and was always dependent on subsidies[11].

After the work was suspended, the smeltery consigned 3000t zinc, 2000t lead, 300t cadmium and other highly toxic materials eg. mercury in the ground[13]. These brownfields were a high danger to the groundwater quality.

Duisburg's government had to intervene.

---

12 Panning, Nierhoff, Hydr. Geologen und Ingenieure
13 Ahlers A 2008

3.2.2 Ways of fighting the Groundwater Threat of the Brown fields

In July 2006 measures were taken to fight the threats to the environment. The main aim was the liquidation of the most urgent toxic substances that had to be stopped from being flushed to the groundwater by rainwater.

When analyzing the ground, workers came to the conclusion that the slag which had been burried everywhere, contained way too much heavy metals to leave it in the ground. It had to be removed.

So the department for environmental issues of Duisburg (Amt für Umwelt und Grün) and the district council of Düsseldorf (Bezirksregierung Düsseldorf) decided on a plan that specified how to solve the problems concerning environment.

At first ca. 23.000t high toxic soil was transported away and disposed. On the entire area at least 2m depth of the ground were dug out and disposed. Workers permanently took samples of the ground and dug until they reached soil that was unobjectionable. In some places the workers even dug to a depth of 9m.

Highly toxic soil was transported to an extern disposal whereas less burdened material was recycled and reused to fill up parts of the area again. In December 2007 the site was finished and ready for further steps in the transformation to the Angerpark.

Soil from the Berzelius area and from other places e.g. From the Project "Parallelkanal" in Duisburg Wedau was formed to a height of 33m (65m over the sea level) and the shape of the later Heinrich-Hildebrand-Höhe.

To protect the groundwater from the remaining heavy metals in the ground, a 2,5mm thick foil was inserted in a depth of 3m. The foil was weatherproof, long lasting and covered an area of 140.000m² when it was finished in July 2007. In July 2007 also the topping-out ceremony took place. After the ceremony the acclivity was elevated once more to a total height of 67m over sea level.

For drainage reasons a layer of easy penetrable material was placed on the foil. So the rainwater could flow down without any harm to the edifice. Trenches were built along the footpath (see Fig. 2), that lead helical to the top of Heinrich-Hildebrand-

Höhe, to simplify the flow of the rainwater to two rain storage reservoirs. The reservoirs had a connection to the river Anger that was used to dispose of the water.

The protection of the groundwater and the stratification of the acclivity caused costs of eight million Euros[2].

3.2.3 Ways of attracting visitors

To make the Heinrich-Hildebrand-Höhe (see Fig. 14) and the surrounding Angerpark more attractive for visitors multiple measure were taken. A 2,7km road network consisting of asphalt was built (see Fig. 15). It circles the base of acclivity and leads helically to the top. In the green areas around the Höhe there is another kilometer of road made of gravel (see Fig. 19).

Park benches (see Fig. 16) can be found in many places of the Angerpark to offer a place for relaxing and watching the landscape.

To improve the outer appearance of the park multiple plants were cropped. All in all 300 higher trees and 55.000 young smaller plants were dibbled. The ground was vegetated by a mixture of different herbage[11].

Along the road system there are multiple information panels (see. Fig. 16) that offer facts about the landscape, land use of the region and the origin of the dump's name (Heinrich Hildebrand was a local historian that published multiple books about the history of Duisburg-Wanheim).

All these measures added up to costs of two million Euro[11].

The final completion will be achieved in 2010 when an 18m high illuminated sculpture of the shape of a roller coaster will be built onto (see Fig. 18) the Heinrich-Hildebrand-Höhe. The jury of a sculpture competition decided in favor of the roller coaster sculpture because it made the Angerpark a "place of visual and communicative pleasure" ("Ort des visuellen und kommunikativen Vergnügens") [14]

The artwork will cost 600.000€ and will be finished in 2010 on the occasion of the "Kulturhauptstadt Essen" festival that will take place in the Ruhr Area.

---

14   Ahlers B 2009

4 Conclusions

4.1 RheinPark

The parts of RheinPark that are finished yet can already now be seen as a success. In the summer many visitors come to relax on the benches at the Rhine or to promenade through the park. Especially the sports facilities are frequently used and particular the skating half pipe bestows Duisburg visitors from throughout the region.

A disadvantage of the park is the missing gastronomy. Many visitors of the park complain about the missing ability to take a drink or have a snack.

And there are even stronger problems. Due to vandalism one can hardly ever see all the lanterns glow at night (see Fig. 6). Also destroyed glass bottles can be found in many places due to the close location to the disco "Pulp", even on playgrounds for small children. Furthermore because of vandalism the establishment of a provisorily kiosk failed (see Fig. 12). Other objects that suffer from vandalism are fixing facilities for the trees (see Fig. 7).

To sum up the advantages and disadvantages of Rheinpark it can be said, that RheinPark is a success with vandalism, gastronomy and waste problems.

4.2 Heinrich-Hildebrand-Höhe

Concerning the environmental protecting function the project can be seen as a success. To date no toxic substances were flushed into the ground water.

However no one can say how long lasting the foils really are. Eventually they will become penetrable and the heavy metals will be flushed into the groundwater anyway. The reparation costs for a destroyed foil will be high. But regarding the fact, that there was no other possibility than the one that was done, no one can complain about this future-problem.

Concerning the Heinrich-Hildebrand-Höhe being a recreational area I would not call the project a success. One can hardly see anyone visiting the dump due to the missing features that could be interesting. The sculpture that will be built on the hill in 2010 could change this state as the consequence of the fact that the dump will look much more interesting and will be viewable from a longer distance.

Summarizing it can be said that Heinrich-Hildebrand-Höhe was a success for the environment but has increase in interestingness to really attract a considerable number of visitors.

4.2 Aftermath for Duisburg and its Inhabitants

Due to an enhanced spectrum of leisure amenities and sports possibilities in Duisburg, its attractiveness increased. People that were used to only few green zones, especially in Duisburg Hochfeld can now relax in the new RheinPark, enjoying nature and industrial history at one time.

Also the danger of polluted drinking water by vacant industrial facilities has been taken away at least in Duisburg Wanheim-Angerhausen. That again increases the attractiveness of Duisburg and calms down worried people.

As Duisburg is one of the cities which will participate in the "Kulturhauptstadt RUHR 2010"-festival, Projects like Rheinpark, with a connection of entertainment and historical background, will attract many visitors due to industrial history being the main topic of the festival. Sights like RheinPark will also improve Duisburg's image by showing visitors the creativity and skill concerning the handling with industrial history in front of a current background. The sculpture that is planned on Heinrich-Hildebrand-Höhe will also be a considerable attraction.

However a problem that RheinPark could implicate are the possibly high follow-up costs caused by vandalism, which is a huge problem in the park. These costs can increase the city's anyway high deficit. Employing some night guards could possibly solve this problem.

Recapitulatory it can be said that the projects, in particular RheinPark, are definitely a success for Duisburg due to its image improving and living standard increasing effects.

5. Material

Source: Lukas Fiedler 2009

5.1 RheinPark

Fig. 2: Skate park

Fig. 2: Climbing wall on a industrial reminder

Fig. 3: Playground

Fig. 4: ArcelorMittal Hochfeld GmbH

Fig. 5: Water tower

Fig. 6: Meadow plateaus and destroyed lanterns

Fig. 7: Trees with destroyed fixing facilities

Fig. 8: Pedestrian bridge over railway

Fig. 8: Preserved undercrossing

Fig. 9: Beach

Fig. 11: Lettering „Duisburg am Rhein"

Fig. 12: Sign informing about the reason
for the kiosk's closing: vandalism
and thievery

Zone 1	
Location	Inside building area
Use	Mainly residential function, service function possible
Construction	Two to four stories, single buildings
Kind of Building	Twin houses, villas, terrace houses
Zone 2	
Location	Edges of building area near main streets
Use	Mixed functions: business, service, residential, gastronomy
Construction	Up to six stories, closed buildings
Kind of Building	Penthouse like architecture
Zone 3	
Location	Edged of building area in the south west and north west
Use	High class mixed function: services for business customers, hotels, company headquarters, business, gastronomy, high class housing
Construction	More than 6 stories, open construction
Kind of Building	Stand-alone buildings, penthouses

Fig. 13: Planned zones for land use in RheinPark
Source of Data: Stadt Duisburg 2005

5.2 Heinrich-Hildebrand-Höhe

Fig. 14: Heinrich-Hildebrand-
Höhe from the east

Fig. 15: Helical road with trench

Fig. 16: Benches and information panel
on the top

Fig. 17: Rain water storage reservoir with
the river Anger in the background

Fig. 18: Area on the top

Fig. 19: Road System

6 Bibliography

Ahlers *A*, **Martin**: Wanheim atmet auf [online]. November 2008.
http://www.derwesten.de/nachrichten/staedte/duisburg/2008/11/7/news-89142295/detail.html 10.11.2009

Ahlers *B*, **Martin**(2009): Achterbahn krönt Halde. In: WAZ-Mediengruppe: West-deutsche Allgemeine Zeitung 25.09.2009

Ausschuss für Öffentlichkeitsarbeit der Niederrheinischen Industrie und Han-delskammer Duisburg – Wesel – Kleve (1987): Der Niederrhein – Wirtschafts- und Lebensraum. Kevelaer/Duisburg: Buzton & Bercker GmbH, Mercator Verlag, Verlag Fachtechnik

Duisburg.de *A*: RheinPark Duisburg [online]. September 2008.
http://www.duisburg.de/micro/eg-du/projekte_rheinpark/projekt_rheinpark.php .
27.11.2009

Duisburg.de *B*: RheinPark Duisburg [online]. unknown date of compose.
Http://www.rheinpark-duisburg.de/ . 01.12.2009

Fuchs, Martina (1999): Werkstatt für die Zukunft von Industrieregionen. In: Just, Peter: Praxis Geographie. Heft 10/1999. Braunschweig, Bildungshaus Schul-buchverlage. Seite 46

Gatermann, Harald: Innehafen Duisburg [online]. Unknown date of compose.
Http://www.hochschule-bochum.de/fb1/af-iba/042-innenhafen.htm . 06.12.09

Heid, Ludger; Kraume Hans-Georg; Lerch, Karl; Milz, Joseph; Pietsch, Hart-mut; Tromnau, Gernot; Vinschen, Klaus Dieter (1996): Kleine Geschichte der Stadt Duisburg. 4. Auflage. Duisburg: Walter Braun Verlag

Hofritz Jutta: Luxusgut Stahl [online]. Dezember 2004.
http://www.zeit.de/2004/50/ThyssenKrupp . 27.11.2009

Ministerium für Städtebau und Wohnen, Kultur und Sport des Landes Nordrhein-Westfalen: Geschichte der Bauausstellung: Daten und Fakten [online].
unknown date of compose. http://www.iba.nrw.de/iba/main.htm . 06.12.09

Müller, Gloria: Duisburg-Rheinhausen [online]. August 2000. http://www.leg-as.de/fileadmin/leg-nrw.de/Gesellschaften/LEG_Arbeitsmarkt-_und_Strukturentwicklung/referenzen/6/downloads/rheinhausen.pdf 10.11.2009

Panning, Ralf; Nierhoff, Rolf; Hydro. Geologen und Ingenieure (unknown date of compose): Von der Metallhütte zum Angerpark. In: Stadt Duisburg, Der Oberbürgermeister, Amt für Umwelt und Grün: Broschüre

Roden, Günther (1975): Geschichte der Stadt Duisburg I – Das alte Duisburg von den Anfängen bis 1905, Duisburg: Braun

Stadt Duisburg: RheinPark Duisburg [online]. September 2005. http://www.gfw-duisburg.de/immobilien_center/investorslounge/index.php 27.11.2009